EXPLORATION THROUGH THE AGES

THE EXPEDITIONS OF
AMUNDSEN

Richard Humble

Illustrated by
Andrew Aloof

Franklin Watts
London · New York · Sydney · Toronto

© 1991 Franklin Watts

First published in Great Britain
in 1991 by
Franklin Watts
96 Leonard St
London
EC2A 4RH

First published in the United
States by
Franklin Watts Inc
387 Park Avenue South
New York, N.Y. 10016

First published in Australia by
Franklin Watts Australia
14 Mars Road
Lane Cove
NSW 2066

UK ISBN: 0 7496 0710 6

A CIP catalogue record for this
book is available from the British
Library.

Designer: Ben White

Editor/Picture Researcher:
Sarah Ridley

Illustrations: Andrew Aloof,
Hayward Art Group

Consultant: John Robottom

Photographs: Martyn Bramwell
30; British Antarctic Survey/M R
A Thomson 29t; Erik and David
Hosking 28; Anne Christine
Jacobsen 15, 17, 19; The
Illustrated London News Picture
Library 26; Norsk
Sjofartsmuseum, Oslo, 4, 5, 8-9,
27; Norway Polarskipet FRAM,
Oslo 7, 14, 20, 23, 24, 29b;
Popperfoto 18, 22.

Printed in Belgium

Words in bold appear in the glossary.

Contents

The call of the Arctic

Roald Engebreth Gravning Amundsen was born near Christiania (modern Oslo) in Norway on 16 July 1872. His father was a prosperous Norwegian sea captain and ship-owner with his own small fleet of sailing ships, and Roald was the youngest of four sons.

As a boy Roald spent much time in the family shipyard, learning how wooden ships and their rigging worked. From an early age he was drawn to the idea of a life at sea. However, in 1886 his father died and his mother decided that he should study to become a doctor after he'd finished school.

Roald's other great love was skiing, Norway's national sport; he had been taught to ski as soon as he could walk. Aged 17, he joined the cheering crowds in Christiania which gave a hero's welcome home to Fridtjof Nansen in 1889. A pioneer of mountain skiing, Nansen had become Norway's first Polar hero by making the first crossing of Greenland's **ice-cap**, with five companions. Nansen's feat inspired Amundsen and three school-friends to make their first long winter skiing trip into the Norwegian mountains.

In July 1890, Amundsen reluctantly began to study medicine in Christiania. However, he had already decided to become a Polar explorer, for which he must first qualify as a ship's captain. So, after his mother died in September 1893, he abandoned medicine and joined the sealing-ship *Magdalena* to gain sea experience. Amundsen hated the butchery of sealing, but this tough voyage (March-August 1894) gave him experience of life in the ice-pack of the Arctic Sea.

▷ Photograph of Amundsen, aged 25. Tall, tough, and wiry, he set himself high fitness standards which his early skiing expeditions in Norway did much to build. When examined for his seven months' military service in the summer of 1895, Amundsen's muscles astonished the doctor.

He was never a natural student; the school exams which he had to take were a struggle for him. But he was always quick to learn from his own mistakes and profit from the experience of others.

▷ *Magdalena* was a typical Norwegian **sealer**, with a tough wooden hull built to stand up to the pressure of the ice.

▽ Waves crash across the heeling deck of the sealing-ship *Magdalena* during Amundsen's first voyage to the Arctic (1894), when he sailed in the crew as an ordinary seaman.

First Antarctic winter

After his voyage in *Magdalena*, Amundsen made other voyages aboard ships of the family fleet, building up his sea time until he qualified as mate in 1895.

In 1893, Nansen had sailed on a new expedition in the specially-built wooden ship *Fram*. He planned to use the slow drift of the Arctic ice and become deliberately frozen in to drift with the ice, hopefully as far as the North Pole. Though he failed in this, *Fram* survived and Nansen made an epic journey with sledges, dogs and skis across the Arctic ice, getting 274 kilometres (170 miles) closer to the Pole than had ever been reached before. Nansen's exploits encouraged a new interest in Polar exploration, in which Amundsen was now to take part.

In 1896, the Belgian officer Adrien de Gerlache bought the Norwegian sealer *Patria* (renamed *Belgica*) for an expedition to Graham Land in the Antarctic. Volunteering to serve without pay, Amundsen joined de Gerlache's expedition as second mate, and *Belgica* sailed for the Antarctic in October 1897.

Among the expedition members was Dr Frederick Cook, who had travelled in north Greenland in 1892 with the American explorer Robert Peary. Amundsen learned much from Cook about Polar equipment, notably how **Inuit** (Eskimo) fur clothing was better than any made in Europe for keeping out severe cold. After *Belgica* arrived off Graham Land in January 1898, Amundsen made several trips ashore. These taught him how quickly men become exhausted when hauling heavy sledges in freezing temperatures. Amundsen never forgot this experience when the time came for him to plan his own expeditions.

On 2 March 1898, *Belgica* was allowed to become frozen in by the **pack-ice**. Now de Gerlache's men became the first to endure the six-month ordeal of an Antarctic winter, when the Sun disappears for two months. One man died from **scurvy**, caused by lack of fresh food. Those who came off best, like Amundsen, listened to Cook and fought off scurvy by eating fresh seal and penguin meat.

When the Sun finally returned on 23 July, Amundsen's hair had turned grey and one of the Norwegian crewmen had gone mad. After many disappointments, *Belgica* eventually broke free of the ice in March 1899, with Amundsen returning to Norway in May of that year.

△ The first ship ever to survive an Antarctic winter. *Belgica* in the pack-ice, with every rope of her rigging glistening with ice, photographed during the long Antarctic winter by Dr Frederick Cook.

▷ On 26 January 1898, Amundsen landed on an island off Graham Land to try his Norwegian skis. This made him probably the first man ever to ski on the solid land of the Antarctic continent.

North
Magnetic
Pole

Canada

Nansen
1888

Greenland

Ellesmere
Island

Alaska

Iceland

Peary, 1909

Bering Strait

ARCTIC OCEAN

North
Pole

Norway

Spitzbergen

Franz Josef
Land

Novaya
Zemlya

Russia

Amundsen in *Gjøa*, 1903-6
Nansen in *Fram*, 1893-1896

△ The Arctic regions,
showing the three-year drift
in Polar ice made by Nansen
in *Fram*, and Amundsen's
North-West Passage route.

◁ December 1900: an
important meeting. In
Nansen's study, Amundsen
explains his plan to find the
position of the North
Magnetic Pole, so winning
the great Arctic explorer's
valuable support.

Conference with Nansen

After returning from the *Belgica* voyage, Amundsen worked hard to qualify for his Master's Certificate. He served the required sea time in another Amundsen family ship, the *Oscar*, on a voyage to Pensacola in Florida. Here he bought a load of tough, elastic hickory wood, ideal for making skis and sledges, and had it shipped to the warehouse of his brother Gustav in Christiania. Amundsen was certain that it would prove useful for a future Polar expedition. (And so it did. Eleven years later, some of this hickory would help carry Amundsen and his men to the South Pole and back.)

By April 1900 Amundsen had decided what his own first Arctic expedition should be. The ice-bound route of the **North-West Passage**, leading from the Atlantic Ocean to the Pacific, had been discovered from the land after several 19th century expeditions. However, no ship had yet managed to force a way through the ice and sail the Passage. Amundsen was determined to be the first to do it.

To raise enough money for the expedition, Amundsen needed to set an important scientific goal for it. He decided to search for the North **Magnetic Pole**: that point in the Arctic, hundreds of kilometres from the "true" North Pole at Latitude 90 **Degrees** North from the Equator, to which all magnetic compasses point. To learn how to make accurate magnetic observations, Amundsen spent 40 days of hard study under the guidance of Professor Georg Neumayer at the German Maritime Institute in Hamburg.

Even more important than the approval of scientists was support for the expedition from Nansen, the giant of Polar exploration. Amundsen visited Nansen in December 1900 to explain his plan, and the meeting went well. Nansen willingly gave his approval for an expedition to the North Magnetic Pole. Now it was up to Amundsen to raise the money, buy a ship, and recruit the men he needed for his expedition.

Amundsen soon found the ship he wanted. This was the *Gjøa*, a Norwegian wooden fishing boat: 29 years old (his own age) but tough and sturdy. He raised the money to buy *Gjøa* by selling his entire share in the family business. The real work of fitting out the ship and finding the men to sail with him could now begin.

▽ The most famous Polar exploration ship of all: *Fram* ("Forward"), a three-masted wooden schooner of 402 tons with an auxiliary engine, launched in October 1892. *Fram* was the first ship designed and built to winter in the Polar ice. Her rounded hull stood up well to ice pressure which has crushed and sunk many bigger ships, even vessels made of steel. Here she is frozen into the ice-pack during Nansen's famous drift across the Arctic Ocean in 1893-1896.

Learning from the Inuit

Though a sound enough ship, *Gjøa* needed both an engine and an outer cover on the hull to stand up to the ice and move through it. The cost of these improvements, and of the other equipment needed for the expedition, put Amundsen deep into debt; only success and fame could save him from ruin.

At last, on 16 June 1903, *Gjøa* sailed from Norway with her crew of seven: Amundsen, Godfred Hansen, Anton Lund, Helmer Hanssen, Peder Ristvedt, Gustav Wiik, and Adolf Lindstrom, the excellent cook and handyman from Nansen's *Fram*.

Amundsen planned to spend at least two winters in the Arctic. The age-old experience of the Inuits would help his men to survive where larger European expeditions had starved, sickened, and died. Amundsen and his men were equipped with reindeer-skin protective clothing, boots and mittens, as worn by the Lapps of Arctic Norway. They intended to rely on hunting and eating fresh meat to resist scurvy. They would learn the art of sledge-dog travel and survival skills, like **igloo**-building, from the local Inuits they met.

After stopping at Godhavn, Greenland, to take on sledges, dog teams, and kayaks, *Gjøa* headed west to Lancaster Sound, the

▷ "Driving school" at Gjøahavn in the winter of 1903-4; the Netsiliks teach Amundsen and his men how to drive a dog team. For Amundsen, the great discovery was that dog teams need regular rest periods, and work hardest when chasing a man on skis out in front.

Atlantic entrance to the North-West Passage. On 23 August Amundsen turned south and entered Peel Sound: the inlet leading south to the only recorded location of the North Magnetic Pole, reached in 1831 by Sir James Clark Ross of Britain. This was on the Boothia Peninsula, the most northern point of the North American continent.

Passing between Boothia and King William Island, *Gjøa* had to survive fog, storms, and near shipwreck on a reef. Then, on 9 September, Amundsen found what he had been looking for: a sheltered bay on the south coast of King William Island. Here he anchored *Gjøa* close to the shore and waited for the winter ice to freeze her in, which had happened by 3 October. He called his base Gjøahavn – "Gjøa Harbour". This would be home for the next 22 months.

By the end of October 1903, with the Arctic winter biting deeper and deeper, Amundsen and his men had made friends with the local Netsilik Inuits. They spent a hard-working winter, learning how to build igloos and trading with the Netsiliks for Inuit clothing. Above all they learned the tricky art of dog team driving, preparing for the search for the Magnetic Pole that would begin with the coming of spring, April 1904.

The North-West Passage

On 6 April 1904, Amundsen set off with Peder Ristvedt and two sledge-dog teams to cover the 145 kilometres (90 miles) between Gjøahavn and the North Magnetic Pole. They used depots of food and fuel, set out in the previous month, to supply their needs.

From the Inuits, Amundsen had learned not to hurry or over-strain himself, thus avoiding sweating and loss of body temperature. He now knew that Inuit sledge dogs are not domestic pets but half-wild. A dog which went sick, or refused to work, was shot and fed to the others.

Travelling in easy stages, they made steady progress. On 26 April they reached the position of the Magnetic Pole reported by Ross, only to find that it had moved. Scientists had suggested that the Earth's

magnetic poles do move; now Amundsen became the first to prove that this is indeed true.

Amundsen and Ristvedt spent three weeks trying to fix the precise point of the Magnetic Pole with their instruments. Then the food safety limit which Amundsen had carefully set was reached, and they headed back to Gjøahavn. This they reached on 27 May, having been away for seven weeks. Amundsen's final calculations showed that they had missed the North Magnetic Pole by only 48 kilometres (30 miles).

For the second Arctic winter Amundsen hoped to make another attempt on the Magnetic Pole, but now had only enough dogs for one party. These he gave to Godfred Hansen and Ristvedt, who made a 1,290-kilometre (800-mile) journey from

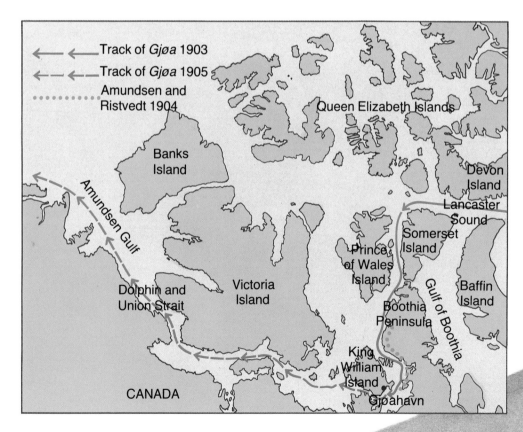

Track of *Gjøa* 1903
Track of *Gjøa* 1905
Amundsen and Ristvedt 1904

Queen Elizabeth Islands

Banks Island

Amundsen Gulf

Devon Island

Lancaster Sound

Somerset Island

Prince of Wales Island

Baffin Island

Dolphin and Union Strait

Victoria Island

Gulf of Boothia

Boothia Peninsula

King William Island

CANADA

Gjøahavn

◁ How Amundsen conquered the North-West Passage: the track of *Gjøa* through the narrow, ice-choked straits between the Canadian Arctic islands. By heading well to the south, Amundsen found open water where no ship had ever sailed.

▷ Triumph! *Gjøa* meets the American whaler *Charles Hansson* at sea on 26 August 1905. "Are you Captain Amundsen?" asked the American captain, to Amundsen's great surprise.

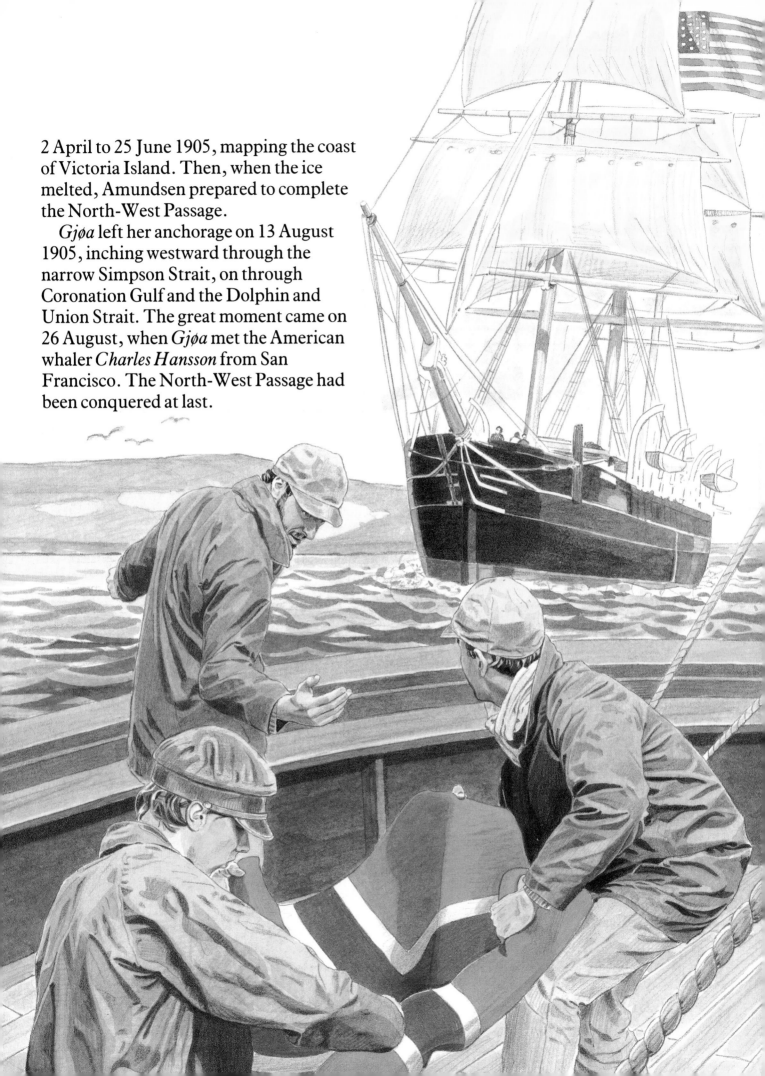

2 April to 25 June 1905, mapping the coast of Victoria Island. Then, when the ice melted, Amundsen prepared to complete the North-West Passage.

Gjøa left her anchorage on 13 August 1905, inching westward through the narrow Simpson Strait, on through Coronation Gulf and the Dolphin and Union Strait. The great moment came on 26 August, when *Gjøa* met the American whaler *Charles Hansson* from San Francisco. The North-West Passage had been conquered at last.

◁ Greenland sledge dogs, sunning themselves on *Fram's* upper deck during the voyage south to the Antarctic in 1910. They lived on a false deck: a great help with the endless job of cleaning up.

△ Compared with the 65 members of Scott's expedition, only 18 men sailed with Amundsen in *Fram*. Here, at the Barrier's edge, the Norwegians work furiously to bring the expedition's dogs and stores ashore.

At Framheim base

For his next expedition, an attempt to reach the North **Geographic Pole**, Amundsen was promised the use of *Fram* by Nansen. However, within three years of returning to Norway from America in 1906, Amundsen was forced to change his plans completely by events in Polar exploration at both ends of the Earth.

In 1902-4, a British naval expedition commanded by Robert Scott had landed in Antarctica and pushed south to Latitude 82 Degrees. In March 1909, the world heard that Ernest Shackleton, one of Scott's officers, had returned from his own expedition after marching to within 156 kilometres (97 miles) of the South Pole. In September came the news that both Dr Frederick Cook (Amundsen's companion in *Belgica*) and Robert Peary of the United States were claiming to have reached the North Pole. Now Scott was preparing another British Antarctic expedition to succeed where Shackleton had so narrowly failed.

Amundsen therefore made the most daring decision of his life. He continued to prepare *Fram* for his next expedition – but she would sail south, not north. With the most expert team of skiers and sledge-dog drivers he could find, he would race Scott to the South Pole.

Keeping his plan secret until Scott's expedition had left Britain, Amundsen landed in Antarctica on 15 January 1911. In the Bay of Whales, after a voyage of 22,520 kilometres (14,000 miles), he set up his base camp, "Framheim", on the edge of the **Ross Ice Barrier**.

▷ On the eve of adventure: Amundsen in his garden in Norway, with Nansen's famous *Fram* anchored offshore. The secrecy behind Amundsen's true destination in 1910 was so tight that a vital trial was conducted in Amundsen's garden. This was the test-building of the special hut, in sections for quick and easy assembly, in which the men of the expedition would spend the Antarctic winter of 1911.

On the Polar plateau

From Shackleton's 1908 expedition, Amundsen knew that the South Pole lay on a high plateau over 1,280 kilometres (800 miles) from Framheim. To get there meant crossing first the vast ice-sheet of the Barrier and then a mountain range, up which **glaciers** offered a choice of routes to the **Polar plateau**.

To make sure of returning safely, Amundsen planned to leave plenty of food and fuel in a line of well-marked depots. By 8 March his sledge teams had planted advance depots at 80, 81, and 82 Degrees South. This was 241 kilometres (150 miles) further south than Scott, whose base at Cape Evans was 700 kilometres (435 miles) west of Framheim in the Bay of Whales.

Throughout the dark winter weeks after the Sun disappeared on 21 April, the Norwegians worked ceaselessly at Framheim. All equipment was checked and overhauled, new light sledges were built from the hickory wood bought by Amundsen back in 1900, and marker-flags made to make the vital depots easy to find. Now Amundsen picked his Polar team: champion skier Olav Bjaaland, Helmer Hanssen from *Gjøa*, Sverre Hassel, and Oscar Wisting.

▷ Amundsen's route to the Pole: from Framheim on the Bay of Whales across the Barrier to the mountains, then up the Axel Heiberg Glacier to the Polar plateau. Unlike Scott, Amundsen had to find a new glacier route through the mountains.

(far right) The Polar plateau at last: 21 November 1911, 32 days out from Framheim. The bloody snow marks the "Butcher's Shop" depot where, according to plan, the Norwegians changed from four sledges to three and shot their 24 surplus dogs. Their bodies would feed the last 18 dogs – and the men – before the last 440 kilometres (274 miles) across the plateau to the Pole.

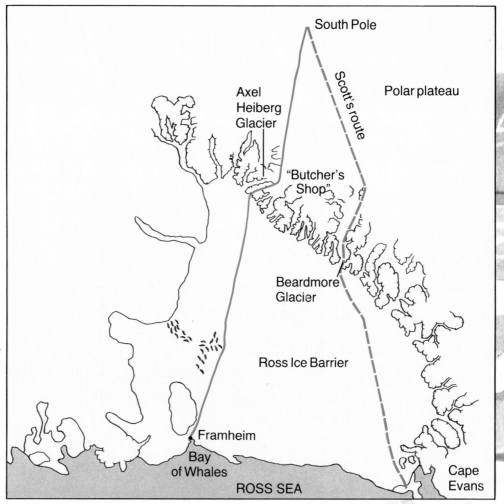

The Sun returned on 24 August, but low temperatures prevented a start until 20 October. They left their depot at 82 Degrees on 7 November with food and fuel for a hundred days, and made steady progress. After leaving more depots at 83, 84 and 85 Degrees, they reached the mountains on 17 November.

Amundsen chose the Axel Heiberg Glacier (named after one of his backers) for the route up to the Polar plateau. Brilliantly led by ski expert Bjaaland, they fought their way up to the Polar plateau on 21 November, and prepared to make the final dash to the Pole.

△ One of Amundsen's dog teams. The Norwegians used the Inuit "fan" hook-up familiar to their Greenland dogs, with each dog on a single trace fanning out from a central hitching-point on the sledge.

The South Pole

To start with, the Polar plateau was hard going. Amundsen's men had to struggle against fog and blizzards which made accurate navigation difficult, frozen snow as hard to ski across as sand, and ice broken by crevasses. On the Barrier they had covered 32 kilometres (20 miles) a day with ease. But it took them ten days to cover the 140 kilometres (87 miles) between the "Butcher's Shop" depot and the smooth ice-sheet which opened before them at 87 Degrees South.

Now able to make good speed, they passed Shackleton's most southerly camp on 8 December, laying their last depot before reaching the Pole itself. They camped on 14 December with only 24 kilometres (15 miles) to go. At 3 o'clock in the afternoon of 15 December 1911, with Amundsen on skis in front of the leading dog team of Helmer Hanssen, the Norwegians reached the South Pole at 90 Degrees South.

Scott was beaten to the Pole because he refused to rely on dogs and skis. He used Siberian ponies to haul supplies across the Barrier, then relied on man-hauling the sledges. When Amundsen reached the Pole, Scott was 579 kilometres (360 miles) behind him, still struggling up the Beardmore Glacier from the Barrier.

Amundsen and his men now made careful observations to confirm that they had really reached the Pole. After making sure of the position and leaving a message in a tent for Scott, Amundsen turned for

◁ Gallant in defeat: the British reach the Pole 33 days after the Norwegians. Standing: Wilson, Scott, Oats; sitting, Bowers and Evans. All died on their dreadful return march. Their notes and this photograph were found in the snowed-up tent of their last camp on the Ross Ice Barrier.

▷ Amundsen's supreme triumph: Norway's flag flies at the South Pole. Amundsen's own camera failed at the Pole, but fortunately Bjaaland's smaller snapshot camera recorded the great moment. The load on this sledge shows the generous amount of supplies carried to the Pole.

▷ At "Polheim", as Amundsen called his South Polar camp, the five men spent nearly three full days taking careful sightings to confirm their position. In the tent, Amundsen left a note for Scott and a letter to King Haakon of Norway.

home on 18 December. Now his careful planning and depot-laying earned a full reward. Amundsen's ration allowance had given him and his men 590 kilograms (1,300 lbs) of food and fuel each – ten times more than Scott's tragic Polar party of five who reached the Pole on 17 January 1912, 33 days after Amundsen. Scott and all his companions died on their return march from hunger, frostbite and scurvy. Amundsen's triumphant party left more than half a ton of unwanted food and fuel in their depots on the Barrier, returning to Framheim in perfect health on 26 January 1912 – ten days before they had been expected.

Flying boats in the Arctic

The South Pole brought Amundsen world fame, but little fortune. Once again, he had many debts to pay off before he could prepare for his next expedition.

Before the North Pole had been reached, Amundsen had hoped to finish Nansen's work by drifting in the Arctic ice as far as the Pole. But *Fram* was now unfit for another Polar voyage, and it took Amundsen until 1918 to prepare another exploration ship, the *Maud*. In July 1918 he set off from Norway to sail *Maud* through the **North-East Passage** along the Arctic coast of Siberia, then drift across the Arctic Ocean from the Bering

Strait. Amundsen thus became the first man to sail both the North-West and North-East Passages, but a broken propeller then made the Polar drift voyage impossible. Amundsen left Oscar Wisting to take *Maud* through the Bering Strait and south to Seattle in the United States.

Always keen to use new technology, Amundsen now decided that the future of Polar exploration lay with aircraft. Though the first flight had only been made in 1903, by the Wright brothers, Amundsen had learned to fly and gained Norway's first civilian pilot's licence in 1914. In 1923, at the age of 50, he prepared

△ One of the Dornier-Wal flying boats in which Amundsen made his dramatic attempt to fly from Spitzbergen to the North Pole in May 1925. This was a venture for which, unlike Amundsen's earlier expeditions, many risks had to be taken. Not enough was then known about the performance of aircraft in Polar regions. Amundsen and his fellow flyers had to find out the hard way, and were lucky to escape with their lives.

to make the first air crossing of the Arctic in a Junkers aircraft, but this crashed before the attempt could be made.

Amundsen was now approached by Lincoln Ellsworth, an American millionaire's son who wanted to become a Polar air explorer. In two metal Dornier-Wal **flying boats**, Amundsen, Ellsworth, and four companions took off from Spitzbergen in May 1925. They made a record flight to just short of 88 Degrees before being forced down on the ice. It took three weeks before one of the Dorniers was made airworthy enough to fly the whole party back to civilisation.

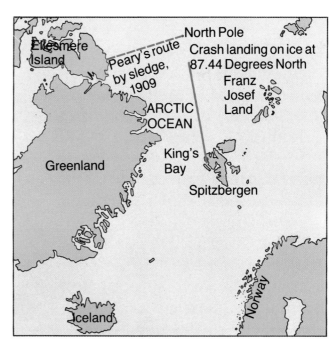

△ Amundsen's flight in the Arctic.
▽ Escape from the ice. Packed into the only Dornier able to fly, Amundsen and his companions begin the flight back to Spitzbergen.

Airship *Norge*

Amundsen was 53 when he made his dramatic escape from the Arctic ice-pack in the summer of 1925. The newspapers made much of the new record set by the flight, and of the fliers' narrow escape. Amundsen found himself back at the centre of world attention as a leading explorer of the new air age.

Despite his two failures with aeroplanes, Amundsen was now determined to make the first air crossing of the Arctic. His new idea was to use a gas-filled **airship**, which seemed less likely to be forced down to earth in the event of engine failure; an airship could simply drift while repairs were made.

By now Ellsworth had inherited his father's fortune, and put up $100,000 towards Amundsen's next flight. He and Amundsen agreed that this should be made in 1926. Commander Richard Byrd of the United States Navy was planning another aeroplane flight to the North Pole but Amundsen, who had already proved that such a flight was possible, was not worried by this. Any success by Byrd would be overshadowed by a flight all the way across the Arctic, for which only an airship appeared suitable at the time.

Amundsen and Ellsworth now set about finding an airship. As all airships were in military service, this meant finding a government prepared to lend one. The search ended in Italy, where the dictator Benito Mussolini agreed to lend the airship *N.1* if its Italian crewmen could

◁ Umberto Nobile, *Norge*'s designer and commander during the North Polar flight of May 1926.

▷ *Norge* arrives at King's Bay, Spitzbergen, after her long flight from Italy via Britain and Leningrad in the Soviet Union.

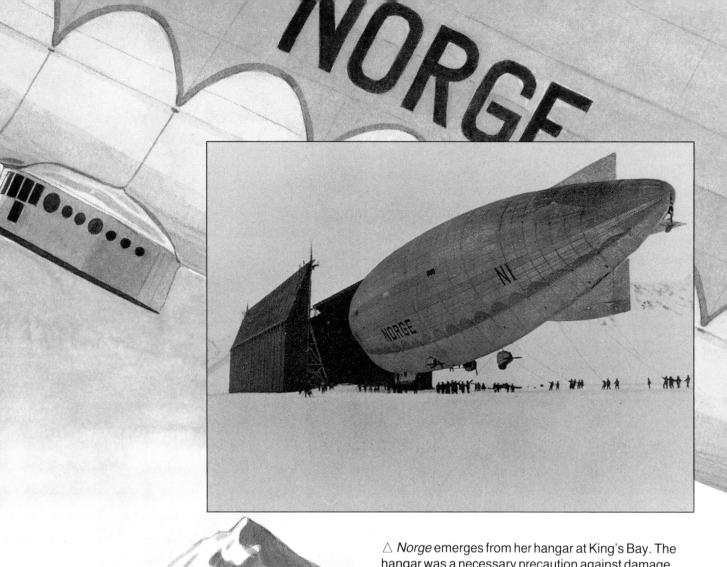

△ *Norge* emerges from her hangar at King's Bay. The hangar was a necessary precaution against damage from the powerful winds of the Arctic during the days of preparation for the trans-Arctic flight.

join the expedition. The airship would be commanded by its designer, Umberto Nobile. In honour of Amundsen's homeland, *N.1* was renamed *Norge* – "Norway".

King's Bay, Spitzbergen, was chosen as the departure-point for the flight, to be known as the "Amundsen-Ellsworth-Nobile" expedition. A special **hangar** was built there to receive *Norge*. She was flown up from Italy by Nobile and his crew, stopping at Pulham airship base in England, and Leningrad in the Soviet Union. By the middle of May 1926, all preparations had been made. The crew and expedition members, assembled at King's Bay, were ready to go.

Over the North Pole

The *Norge* flight was not at all like Amundsen's other expeditions. The most men he had ever taken were the eight of the South Polar expedition. In *Norge*, Amundsen flew with no less than 15 companions. This time he knew, as never before, that he was really only a passenger in a type of craft about which he knew next to nothing. The command and mechanical running of *Norge* were sensibly left to the Italians, who had built her and who knew her best.

Nobile's crew included five Italians, four of whom were mechanics and the fifth a rigger. Apart from Amundsen there were seven Norwegians. These included the faithful Oscar Wisting, who had stood with Amundsen at the South Pole and sailed with him in *Maud*; and Hjalmar Riiser-Larsen, one of the 1925 Dornier party. The Norwegians shared duty at the rudder and elevator controls; Riiser-Larsen and another Norwegian, Emil Horgen, shared the navigating. All orders were given in Italian and Norwegian.

The aim was to fly non-stop across the North Pole to Nome in Alaska. Amundsen was confident that the flight would confirm whether or not there was land in the region of the North Pole, or whether the Pole lay (as it does) in the middle of a frozen ocean.

Norge took off from King's Bay on the morning of 11 May and headed swiftly north, helped by favourable winds. They were lucky. There was no freezing fog, which can make any aircraft too heavy with ice to stay in the air. During the

▷ Earthbound after the triumphant first flight across the Arctic: *Norge*'s cabin beneath the deflating envelopes after the gas-bags were ripped open to let the hydrogen gas escape. Amundsen was full of praise for the skill with which Nobile landed *Norge* at Teller, without the help of a landing-mast or a trained ground crew to secure the ship.

flight, only light damage was caused to *Norge*'s outer skin by ice fragments thrown off by the propeller blades.

At 1.30 am on 12 May *Norge* approached the North Pole, cutting her engines and dropping to 182 metres (600 feet). At the Pole the flags of Norway and Italy were dropped on weighted staffs, and the flight was resumed. Fog over Alaska made navigation difficult. An early landing was advisable, and Nobile brought *Norge* safely to earth at Teller, less than 100 kilometres (62 miles) north-west of Nome, in the evening of 13 May.

△ *Norge*'s track across the Arctic Ocean from King's Bay, Spitzbergen, to the village of Teller on the Alaskan coast.

▽ The scene in *Norge*'s cabin as the flags of Norway and Italy were dropped at the North Pole on 12 May 1926.

Wreckage on a wild sea

After *Norge*'s flight across the Arctic, Amundsen announced that he was going to retire. His fame was at its height, as the first man (with Oscar Wisting) to reach both Poles of the Earth. But there was to be no peaceful old age for Amundsen in his home at Bundefjord.

Amundsen in 1926 still had debts to pay off on both sides of the Atlantic; he had never used exploration to make himself rich. His friends were saddened by a bitter quarrel between Amundsen and Nobile over who deserved most credit for the *Norge* flight, and by the boastfulness of the memoirs which Amundsen published in 1927. Amundsen also felt insulted by the British who, he thought, had never given him full credit for beating Scott to the South Pole.

Then, in May 1928, Amundsen was suddenly called from retirement. On a second airship expedition to the Arctic, Nobile's *Italia* had crashed on the pack-ice north of Spitzbergen. The plight of the

△ The "Red Tent" used by the *Italia* survivors, who were finally rescued by aircraft and the Russian ice-breaker *Krassin*.

▷ When the wreckage from the Latham was found, a float and a fuel tank had clearly been used as rafts. Amundsen and his companions must have fought death to the last.

stranded fliers caught the imagination of the world, and missions were planned to find and rescue the lost Italians. Regretting his quarrel with Nobile, Amundsen at once announced his willingness to join the search. By the middle of June, when a fleet of aircraft and rescue ships was on its way to the Arctic, the French Government had provided Amundsen with a Latham flying boat and pilot.

On 18 June 1928, Amundsen took off for Spitzbergen with two companions. They were never seen again. Months later, wreckage from the Latham was recovered from the Arctic seas. In trying to out-race the other rescuers as he had out-raced Scott in 1911, Roald Amundsen had sacrificed his life.

▽ The last picture of Roald Amundsen, taken just before he took off from Tromso on 18 June 1928. His aircraft was last seen out at sea by a fisherman, disappearing into a bank of fog.

End of an heroic age

In the history of exploration, Roald Amundsen is unique for the list of "firsts" which he achieved. He was a member of the first expedition to survive an Antarctic winter. He was the first to sail both the North-West and the North-East Passages. He was the first to reach both the South Pole and the North. He planned and made the first air crossing of the Arctic Ocean.

Amundsen was always ready to admit how much he owed to the work of others – to Sir John Franklin, who died while discovering the North-West Passage in 1848; and the pioneering trail blazed in the Arctic by Fridtjof Nansen, to name but two. But Amundsen was also remarkable for the method with which he studied all the experience built up by others. Not the least of these lessons were the age-old Polar survival skills of the Inuits, which Amundsen learned and used so well.

The remarkable 30 years which Amundsen shared with Nansen, Peary, Scott, and Shackleton have been called the "Heroic Age" of Polar exploration. Yet Roald Amundsen was never a man who gloried in heroic suffering. Rather than defying Nature, he studied and used it. Amundsen regarded Scott's obsession with man-hauling sledges as crazy, when there was so much evidence of what dog teams and skiers could do. It was ironic, yet somehow right, that at the end Amundsen sacrificed his life while attempting an over-hasty rescue, which others finally achieved.

◁ Scott's base hut at Cape Evans. The hut has been restored and is now a Polar Museum and British Historic Monument. But Amundsen's Framheim hut, built on the edge of the Barrier ice, slid into the sea over 60 years ago.

At Cape Evans, Scott's memorial cross carries the famous lines from Tennyson's *Ulysses*: "To strive, to see, to find, and not to yield." But this quotation was first chosen by Nansen in 1907 – in honour of the conquest of the North-West Passage by Amundsen.

◁ The most famous ship in Polar exploration: the *Fram* of Nansen and Amundsen, today preserved in her building at Bygdøy, Oslo.

△ At the South Pole today. This is the permanently-manned Amundsen-Scott Base, an American base for Antarctic study and research.

Nor did Amundsen cling obstinately to established ways, when science offered new and better tools. Having used skis and sledge dogs with outstanding success, he saw that aircraft were clearly the key to the Polar expeditions of the future. The *Norge* flight of 1926 was more than just another of Amundsen's Polar "firsts". It opened up one of the world's most time-saving international air routes, still in busy use by the jet liners of today.

Amundsen closed his memoirs with these words: "The victory of human kind over Nature is not that of brute force alone, but also that of the spirit."

Glossary

Airship Flying machine kept airborne by bags of gas, such as helium or hydrogen, which are lighter than air. It carries a passenger cabin and is driven by engines.

Degree Measurement of position on the Earth's surface, either north or south of the Equator (degrees of Latitude), or east or west of the Greenwich Meridian (degrees of Longitude). The Equator is at 0 Degrees.

Flying boat Aeroplane with boat-shaped hull and supporting floats, able to take off from, and land on, water. When fitted with wheels, in order to operate from ice or land, flying boats are known as "amphibians".

Geographic Poles Fixed points on the Earth's surface at Latitude 90 Degrees north and south of the Equator.

Glacier Large mass of slow-moving ice that covers vast land areas. There are two main types; valley glaciers which form high up in mountain ranges, and continental glaciers which occur in Polar lands.

Hangar Large shed to protect aircraft from wind and weather.

Ice-cap Type of glacier forming a sheet of permanent ice covering a Polar land-mass, as in Greenland and Antarctica.

Igloo Dome-shaped hut or shelter built

▷ Eighty years after Amundsen's South Polar triumph, British Antarctic Survey members learn the art of driving a dog team.

from blocks of packed snow.

Inuit Correct name for the Eskimo people of the Arctic.

Magnetic Poles Moving points on the Earth's surface, at the northern and southern ends of the Earth's constantly shifting magnetic field.

North-East Passage Sea route between the Atlantic and Pacific Oceans, along the Arctic coast of Russia and Siberia. First sailed by Baron Nordenskiold of Sweden in *Vega* (1878-79).

North-West Passage Ice-choked sea passage between the Atlantic and Pacific Oceans, winding between the islands of Arctic Canada. First sailed by Amundsen in *Gjøa* (1903-6).

Pack-ice Wide areas of ice completely covering the Polar seas, packed together by wind, tides, and currents, and only briefly split by "leads" of open water.

Polar plateau The high, mountain-fringed ice-cap of central Antarctica on which the South Geographic Pole lies.

Ross or **"Great" Ice Barrier** The permanent Antarctic ice shelf stretching from the Ross Sea to the Antarctic mountains. Discovered in 1841 by James Clarke Ross of Britain, it was crossed by Shackleton, Amundsen, and Scott during the attempts to reach the South Pole between 1908 and 1912. Today the Barrier is known as the "Ross Ice Shelf".

Scurvy A weakening and, if not halted, fatal disease caused by lack of fresh food.

Sealer Ship used for the hunting and slaughter of seals.

1773-74 Captain James Cook of Britain makes the first crossing of the Antarctic Circle, sighting the pack-ice of Antarctica.

1831 James Clark Ross of Britain discovers the North Magnetic Pole in the Canadian Arctic.

1845-48 Death of Britain's Sir John Franklin and all his men during the discovery of the North-West Passage.

16 July 1872 Roald Amundsen born near Christiania, Norway.

1897-98 Amundsen sails with de Gerlache's *Belgica* expedition, the first to survive an Antarctic winter.

1903-6 Amundsen, in *Gjøa*, completes the first sailing of the North-West Passage.

1909 American Robert Peary reaches the North Pole.

15 December 1911 Amundsen, with four companions, reaches the South Pole.

1918-19 Failure of Amundsen's attempt to drift across the Arctic Ocean in *Maud*.

1925 Amundsen fails to reach the North Pole with Dornier flying boats.

11-13 May 1926 Amundsen makes first air crossing of Arctic Ocean in Italian airship *Norge*.

June 1928 Death of Amundsen, drowned in the Arctic during the attempted rescue of survivors from the crashed airship *Italia*.

Index

PRINTED IN BELGIUM BY
proost
INTERNATIONAL BOOK PRODUCTION